AF377688

EVERYTHING IN THE UNIVERSE
is UNFINISHED

YOKO ONO

EVERYTHING IN THE UNIVERSE
is UNFINISHED

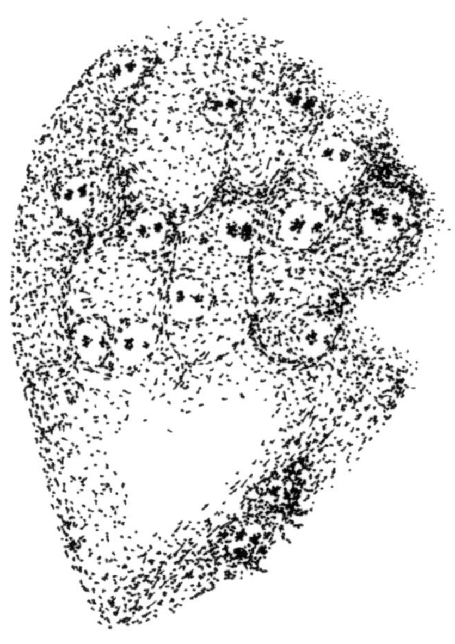

ASK THE UNIVERSE!

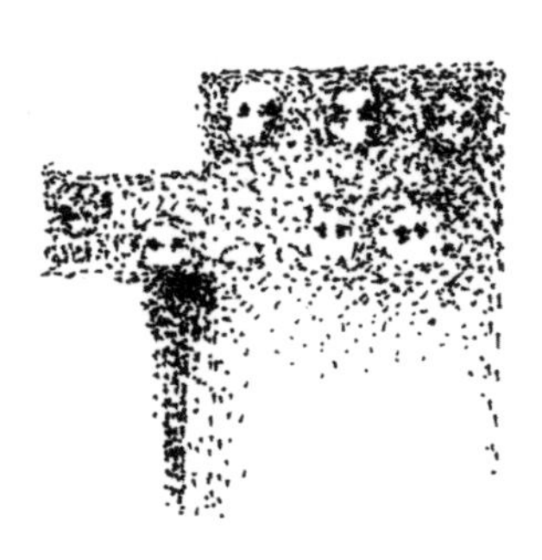

Believe in yourself and you will change the world.

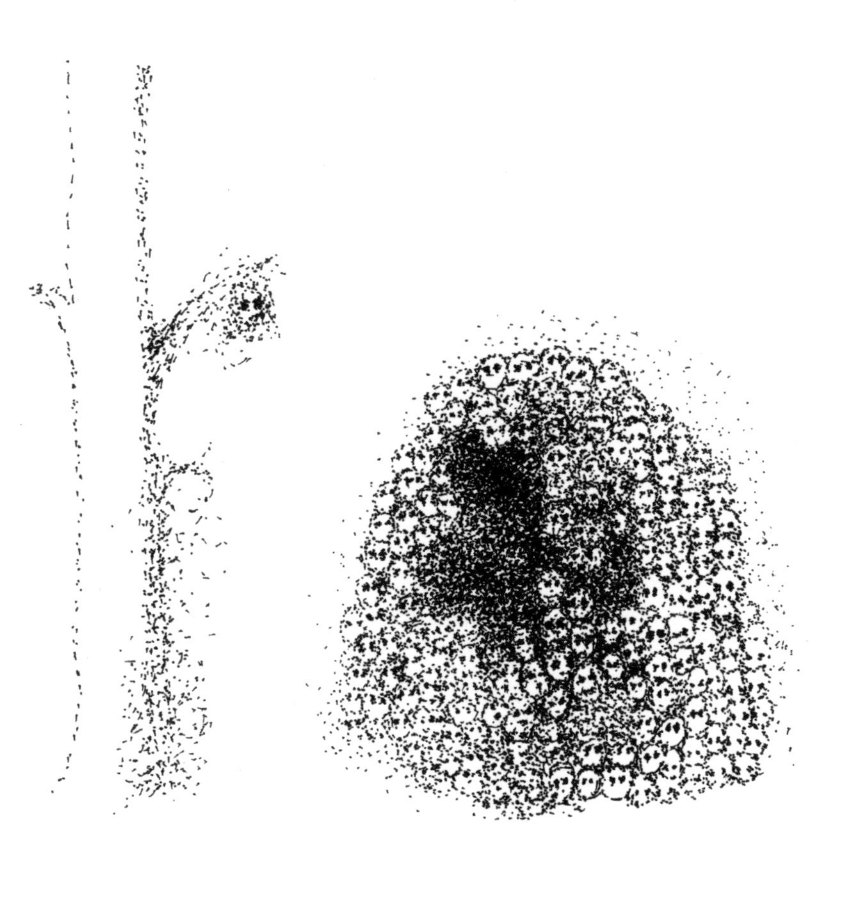

INVISIBLE PEOPLE

Look through the telescopes
for the people
arriving in small boats,
seeking refuge,
from far away wars.

There is the sound of a horn,
tapping of the water against the boats,
and the sound of people
shouting in the distance.

A beautiful sound
was made by all the winds
in the universe.

However, not a shadow of a boat
can be seen
with the naked eye
or through the telescopes.

TWO CANCERIAN PEOPLE IN LOVE

1.   I used to have a crush on Kafka. My mother said:
"Why are you always having a crush on people who died
a long time ago?" I thought of the list of guys I had a crush
on … My mother was right. They were all dead a long,
long time ago … But they were very talented guys.

2.   I always melt when a guy is super-brainy. It seems
that it's not easy to find many super-brainies who are
still alive.

3.   One was Abraham Lincoln. I loved the statue of him
silling on a large chair. I think he was really an honest guy.
That's another thing. Is there a guy who is honest
and also brainy? I thought Lincoln should have resolved
the problem facing him not by creating war, but by
his brainwork. Well, c'est la vie! I say.

4.   I really think guys have different brains from us.
While we are baking chocolate cake for the family,
they are out in the field thinking of how to pull the trigger
faster than the guys in a different uniform. It's only
a uniform, you know. He could have been your mother's
lover who was actually your father. But hey, that doesn't
count, I see.

5.   I bet many guys were shot just for wearing
a different uniform.

6.   I would have worn the enemy's uniform. Easy.
But no man thinks of doing that unless he wants to be
laughed at for being a coward.

7.   How about two thousand men wearing women's
clothes and having great makeup on to approach
the enemy?

8.   They may have done something like that.
But they don't want to bring back home a photograph
of themselves in lacy tops and good-looking skirts.

9.   They say they couldn't do it, because their wives would hate them.

10.   Would we? Even if it meant life or death for them?

11.   I go back to Mozart. He was indeed a first-rate talent. But I didn't have much love for him, because his music was mostly light comedy. Don't get upset I called his music that. I loved talents like Chopin. Chopin was so sensitive and beautiful, you wonder if he wasn't a woman. Yes, he lived with a woman artist—George Sand, who had a man's name but was a genuine woman with big breasts and a very big rubbery body, and she was nuts about him, until he died of consumption. Women love his music. But I couldn't quite get a handle on going nuts for him, since it would have been like barging in on their unusual love affair. Is that what put me off? No, it's her big, big breasts that seem to be suffocating the delicate composer. But he must love all that. Don't you think?

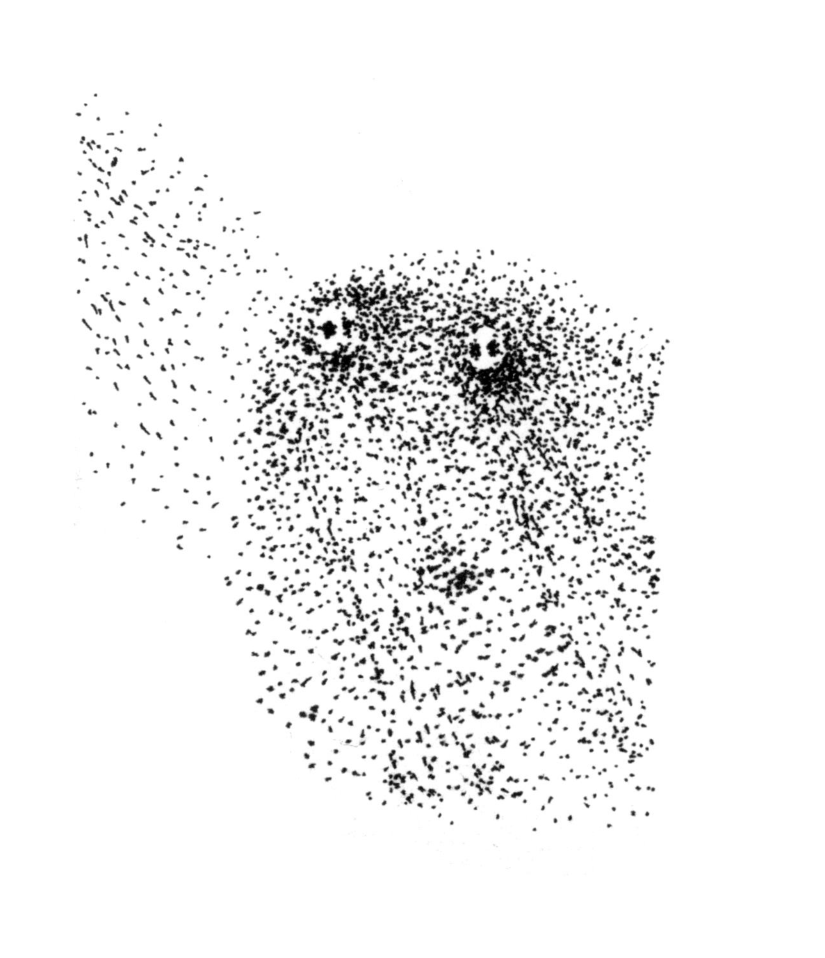

12.   I was invited to a dinner for an artist who is now having
a great show at MoMA. It was nonchalant on the surface,
but top class guests, a who's who of the art world were
all there. I was amazed. "You invited more people this time,
didn't you?" I said. "No, no, no. The number of guests was
exactly the same as your dinner," they told me. "Oh I see."
I didn't quite see, but I decided to shut up. Unless I was
willing to sound like a jealous bitch. I must say we all enjoyed
the dinner. No long speech, no little digs. War Is Over!
might be happening in reality outside the museum. We just
kept applauding the speechmakers. So nobody stood up
and left. The food was impeccable, too. "I enjoyed your show
in Bilbao," somebody came and said to me, "Oh, how nice,
thank you … " "Could I have your photograph with me?
I hope you don't mind…" She said to me. "Of course, not."
I replied. I'm a sitting duck. But it's not as bad as getting
bitten by a mosquito, not knowing if it has the scary disease
they are all talking about. So I accommodate. We stay and
stay. Finally I leave, saying goodbye to each person who sat
around me all night, and wondering if I was leaving at the
right time, or not. Should I have stayed more? …

13.   This is the most enlightened high priest in Asia.
He may not be here for very long. I want to introduce
you to him … Pretty soon, I was invited to the high priest's
temple on a small island. The stillness of the Buddhist
garden mixed with the subtle sounds of the ocean.
A young boy in a simple black and white Buddhist robe
was sweeping the garden. The high priest made tea for
us. Surprised, we just bowed and started to drink the tea.
Silences were so the high priest could give us some
sacred words. The time had come. My heart was beating
fast.

Suddenly, the high priest started to talk. (Yes?)
"That temple has not been there for so long, and now
they are making so much money. I don't know how
they do it. They don't seem to be doing anything more
than what we do, you know. You wonder what we are
doing wrong?" And he laughed a hearty laugh.

I couldn't believe my ears. What happened to the
promised sacred word? After drinking the tea in the way
you are supposed to, we thanked him and left quietly.
Was this a Zen joke? Was he testing us?

14.   It would be good if I could tell you about the very memorable experiences I had in religious organizations in the West. But I don't think I can. That's when I learnt that even though I totally believe in sharing, there are experiences you cannot share.

15.   Women. Poor women! After giving birth to a child, spending nine months of bodily unpleasantness to add another person to this troubled world, we know what is expected of us. We have to have loved the experience. We have to love the stranger called baba or googoo until they grow up into a selfie who is never satisfied with the skimpy love we gave and they have gotten.

Sorry. I said it! But my constant constipation is gone for a good second! You see, honey, your mom wanted to go back to school and brush up her Greek and take off some weight around her tummy. But she hardly had time for anything but to go cuchi-cuchi-coo to you. You were such a cute thing, what else could I have done? I wanted to get the sacred word from the high priest, which might have changed things …

16.   I always lived in desperation. I don't know why …
One day I thought, for my own benefit I should list
the things that are making me desperate. It turned into
a book. David, you just used my list of things … to wipe
yourself, and flushed it! Wasn't it too rough on you?
How could you not notice that it wasn't … what? It was
your revenge on me … so what did I do, or not do. I know
you don't like my cooking … But I can't help that. You
should talk to me sometime … I think sharing information
is a good way to come back to each other … Yes, that's
what they say … I think they have a point …

17.   I don't know. Something is wrong with my life.
So what is it? Oh, no. It's not me, dear. It may be the
Mercury retrograde. But it's awfully long for that, isn't it?
Mercury retrograde and Venus retrograde together?
I never heard of such a thing …

18.   Today's newspaper says 80 percent of our city men
have stomach cancer. And 90 percent of New York City
women have breast cancer. So it's not just me, is it?
We are in the same boat. David, there's something cool

about us having the same disease at the same time,
don't you think? Like you can finally love me again or
something. I feel like I can relate to you better now that
we have the same problem …

19.   David, are you listening? David, David!
(The story is getting rather boring, since the end is
obvious.)
     But if you can save them—and the baby too,
please try and write the rest of the script. There are ten
more chapters to go. Make it positive, "YOU CAN DO IT.
YES, YOU CAN." Let's go!

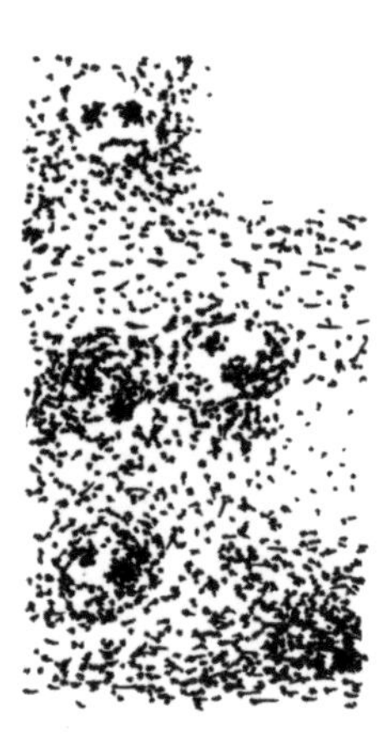

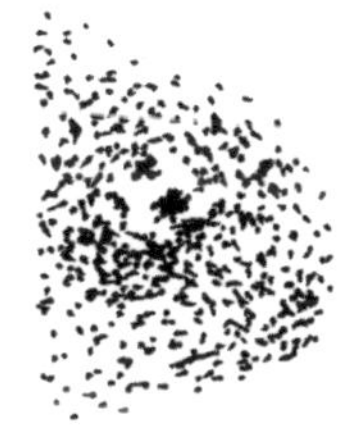

TWO MERCURIAN PEOPLE

I kept cutting my body to the point that finally I saw what it's made of. It was made of clay. That was a relief. It was also painful proof that I was alone. But still something in me was pushing me to open the window. What I see when I open the window is a snowfield. Some were still asleep. I could not wait until he's awake. I was in a total scare. There was no pencil, and what I wrote kept melting. But there was still some " … " in that situation. Is it more, that that woman is cut off? I held my hands, it was so cold. It made me realize that a woman's hand cannot be anything but cold. I cannot be touched by anything. I need to be touched. I will disappear. I realized so many things while I was looking for a hand. It was not as though I wished the hand would hold me. The hand is like an independent warm thing. It was busy looking for something. Am I going to be like this forever? I cannot feel. I hope the body can become supple and alive. I cannot allow myself to disappear before I write and write. The snow keeps falling and I am talking to myself.

Is that a woman's life? I was thinking you may want to hold
onto … At least that will not disappear. The whole body,
the blood of the body. Where did it go? I only hear my son's
breathing. An international woman's day. It's what I wrote.
Even if my whole body is cut off, I hear music. And I have to
write it right away. Life is a woman's life. A man seems to
want their writings. Women seem to not even have a pencil.

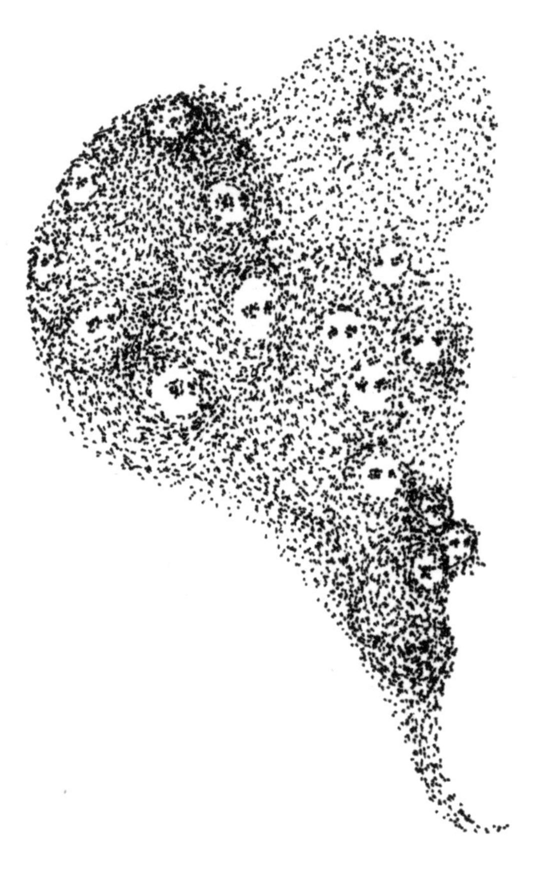

Unfinished Music ...
(Still Searching For Life)

Gaiety
Which does not exist
In my life at this point
Would I like it? If it did?
If I met with it now?
What do I have to go through
To be angry and
Stay in the state of anger.
I'm getting too anemic for it
In fact, I'm getting more and more anemic.

Thousands of ants
Were having a good time
Or a bad time
Who knows
In the end does it matter?
Yes
I think it does matter

My life should be so beautiful
And so precious
It should almost never have an ending
I feel good
That my life is going on

Gaiety of life
The sun was shining
The park was pretty as it can be
Was that the life I lost?

Pain is something that you endure
Yourself
What a joke!
Could I hold onto my energy to do it?
Did somebody say you enjoy things together?

I had a dream
We were definitely together
Tell me about your life,
Are you soaking in the life
Of being thankful

Or not knowing quite what
Pain can be?
Well
I am not as angelic
As some people
Who know how to give forgiveness

In my case
Not to express anger
Is pure laziness
But one day I will
Meet one thing
That will make me stand up again

Yes
All this time
When you have been through so many lives …

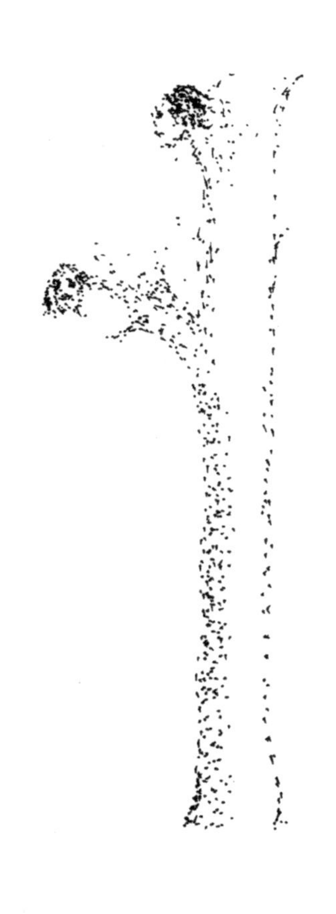

Owl interrupting the work whenever it wishes.

Owl is telling us something.

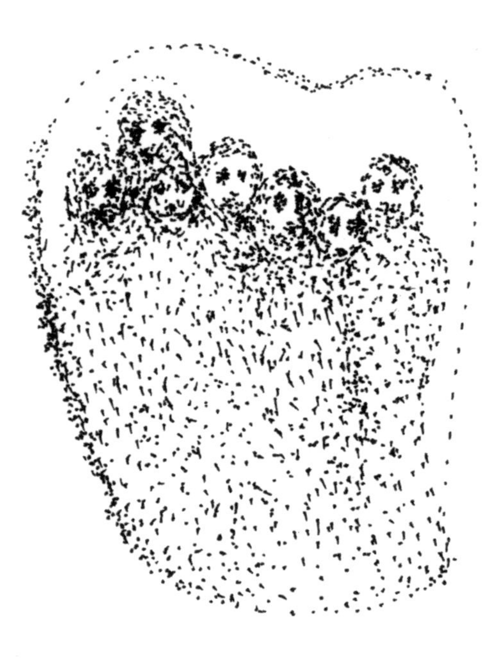

UNFINISHED ROOM

It was great!
It sparkled
With its unfinishedness
In the room of unfinished youth.
It sparkled with unfinishedness.
It sparkled with its unevenness
In the evenness.
I loved your unfinishedness.
Don't ever finish.
I will remember you
Sean
Here is an
Unfinished painting
Put in a room
Called unfinished.

Add what you love about the universe.

What can a pen do?

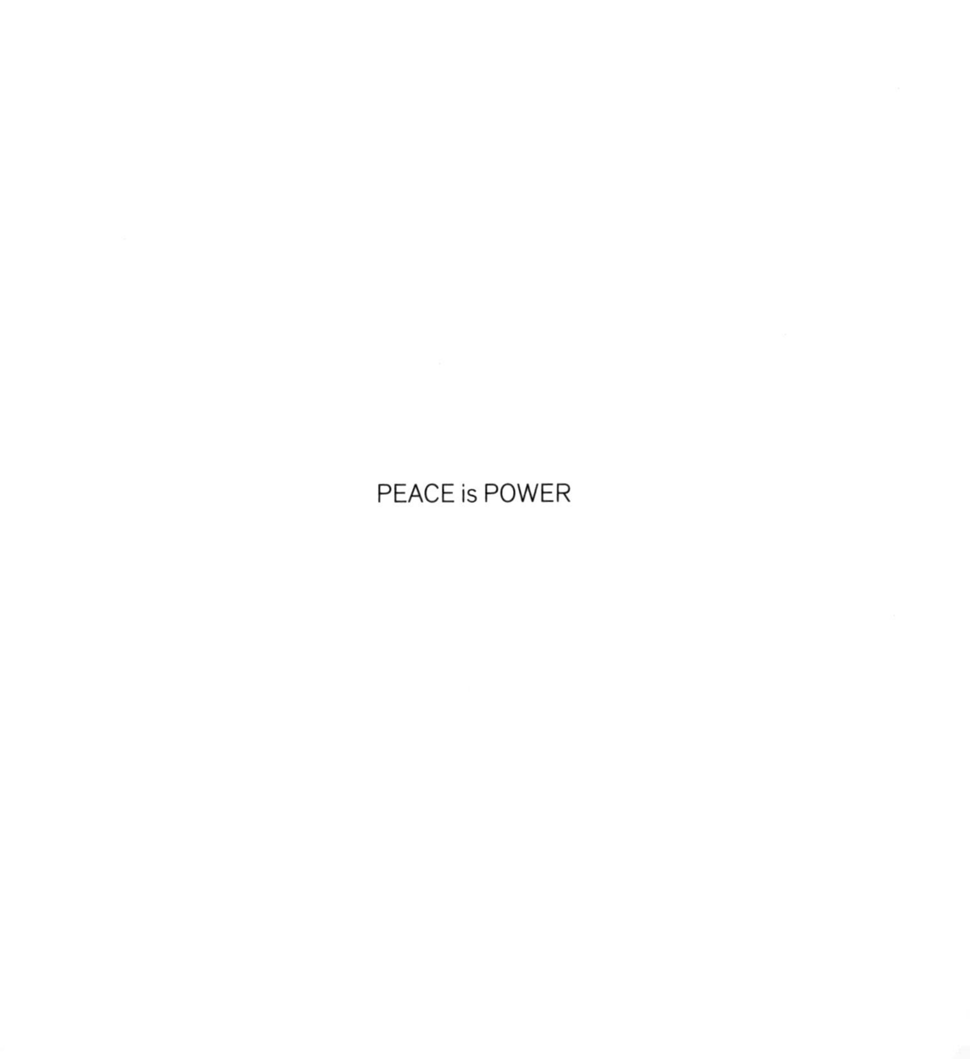
PEACE is POWER

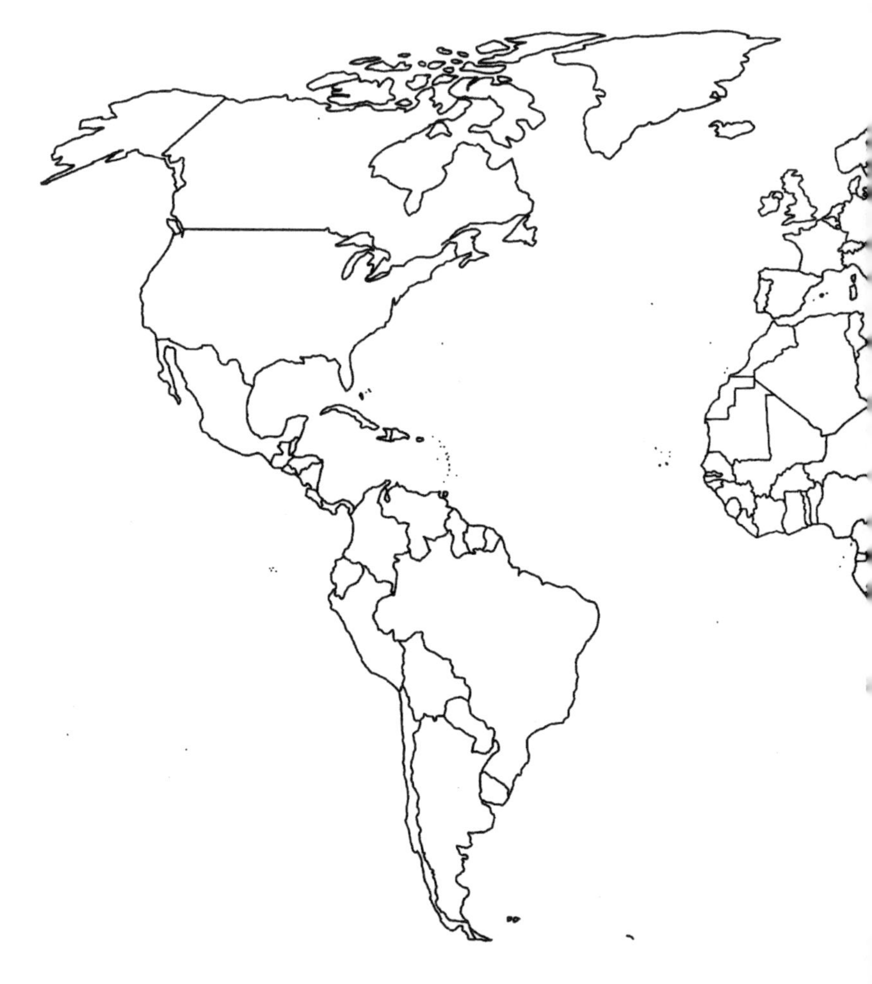

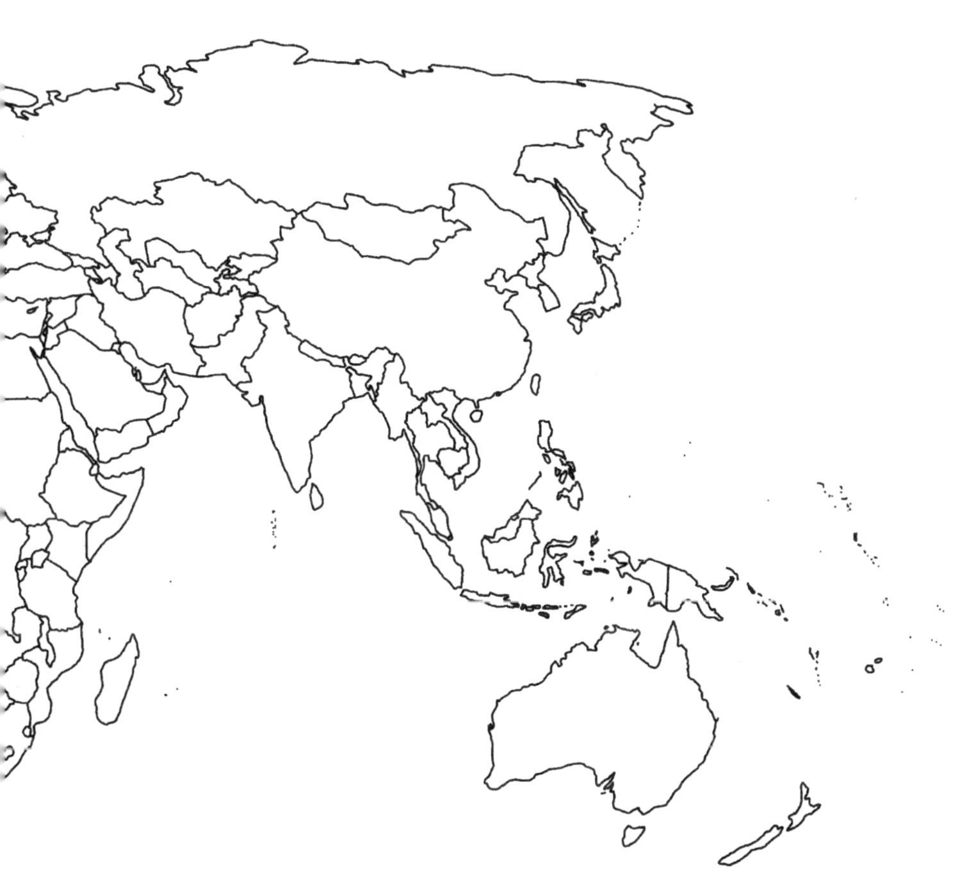

Add color where the world needs peace.

i ii iii

Stamp

This stamp can be used anywhere in the world.

INVITATION TO PEACE!

I'd like to invite you to my home in New York City.

You will have to go to Beijing first. There you will be
inspired and have an exhibit of your work. Take a photo
of yourself and your work.

Then go to the North Pole. There you will see what we are
doing to the white bears. Take a large amount of food
(fishes) otherwise they might think you are the food. Take
a photo of you and the white bears.

From there on you can go to Iceland and Greenland,
which will give you clean pure air, which you wouldn't think
exists on our globe now, but it does. Take a photo of
yourself in those two places and send a postcard with
a little bag of air to your family.

Then make a big turn and go to Auschwitz. There you
will see what we have done as human beings. You will

probably have to stay in Munich one night, otherwise you'd be exhausted, and from Munich, New York City is rather near. Take a photo of yourself in both places and carry it in your heart.

In New York City you can ask people where The Dakota Bar is, and then you will come to my apartment. See you then. We'll be waiting!

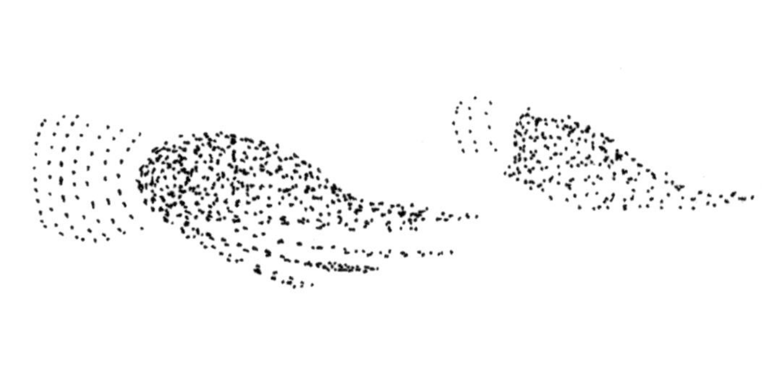

2018 was a great year.

It passed away like the others.

The drawings in this publication are all from
Yoko Ono's "Franklin Summer" series and were realized
in 1994. All the texts were written by Yoko Ono
for this publication between 2016 and 2018.

Editorial Coordination
Connor Monahan
Clément Dirié

Proofreading
Clare Manchester

Design
Michael Sirianni
Nicolas Eigenheer, Nicolas Leuba

Typeface
Theinhardt (www.optimo.ch)

Color Separation & Print
Musumeci S.p.A., Quart (Aosta)

Second edition. First edition published
in 2018.

Published by

JRP|Editions
Rue des Bains 39
CH–1205 Geneva
www.jrp-editions.com

ISBN 978-3-03764-610-6

Printed in Europe

JRP|Editions publications are available
internationally at selected bookstores and
from the following distribution partners:

Switzerland
www.ava.ch

Germany and Austria
gabriele.kern@publishersservices.de

France
www.lespressesdureel.com

UK and other European countries
www.cornerhousepublications.org

USA, Canada, Asia, and Australia
www.artbook.com

Please share where the world needs peace on Twitter, Instagram, and Facebook with #peaceispower.